It's Fun to Paint

PAINTING FOR ENJOYMENT

*By Arnold Blanch
and Doris Lee*

Tudor Publishing Company · New York

ND 1262
B 63

FOREWORD

THIS book is for many people — for many different kinds of people — because in the history of painting, pictures have emerged from all classes of people. The former Prime Minister of England, Winston Churchill, is an amateur painter. There is a little old lady from upper New York State, Grandma Moses, who raised a family and took up painting very late in life. She painted for pleasure and, incidentally, became famous. There are charming and beautiful paintings in Colorado ranch houses, in Negro shacks in South Carolina and in the immaculate drawing room of a well-known corporation lawyer in New York. These are all the results of the enjoyment of painting by self-taught painters.

For you who would like to paint, whoever and wherever you are, this book is offered. To enjoy the experience of painting, you do not have to be an expert. We can all enjoy playing tennis or singing in the moonlight without being Bill Tilden or Lily Pons. You may think you have very little talent, but what of it? Talent is not a thing to be measured or weighed.

The authors of this book make no offer to teach you to paint professionally. We do not believe painting can be taught from a book, but we do believe we can help you to teach yourself to the extent of being able to have a very good time. A highly skilled creative artist usually has behind him many years of complex study and experience, and comprehension of the great traditions of this old and noble profession. Naturally, we cannot attempt to move this mountain, but we shall try to make you familiar with a simple procedure that will encourage you to paint, without fear, anything from an apple to a battle scene. We shall try to show you that your personal or naive qualities can, in your paintings, become a source of artistic charm.

We warn you that painting as an avocation is alluring and seductive. Once you become involved, you neglect your garden, forget your meals, ruin your clothes and, in general, become a family problem. Recently, while in Hollywood, we called on an old acquaintance, Edward G. Robinson, movie actor and art collector. He showed us his beautiful collection, which is hung throughout his house. In one room a luxurious white rug was smeared with yellow paint. Seeing we had discovered his secret, Mr. Robinson admitted he was trying to paint, and said "I love it, but it gets over everything!" Once you begin to paint you will love it too, and even the smell of paint will become exciting like the odor of coffee before breakfast.

In considering the purposes of this book, the authors have hesitated to include reproductions of their own work. We are not completely self-taught painters. Because her method of working is usually simple, direct and logical, my former student and collaborator, Doris Lee, has included two pictures in process, with her own explanations. These reproductions should in no way be considered as formulas or recipes. They are only meant to show a way of treatment that may be helpful to you in the development of your own methods.

In the other paintings reproduced, we have selected examples from many self-taught artists, with interesting variations in subject, time and locale.

ARNOLD BLANCH

CONTENTS

1. TALENT

OF THE 274,995,500 English- speaking people in the world, 274,995,500 have probably said, at least once, "I can't even draw a straight line." This is not so very remarkable, nor would it have been remarkable if Rembrandt could not draw a straight line. If you really did want the line straight, you could go to the 5 & 10 cent store and buy a ruler. A straight line is often a beautiful thing, and so are lines that are not straight. In analyzing this cliché we find it springs from the fear of making a mistake,

Painting by 18 year old boy in Georgia
Collection Lou Block

Painting by 17 year old boy in Texas
Collection Lou Block

and the fear of not doing the orthodox thing. Perhaps to some the straight line is a symbol of the idea that truth is beauty, and there is a subconscious fear of not making something beautiful.

There has been too much dull nonsense written about beauty and truth, so we shall not try to add to it. If there were such absolutes, the painting of all times would be alike, and we should be stuck with one type of Miss America forever. Most painting that conforms to orthodox standards is dull painting, and, as for the fear of making mistakes, that fear is the greatest mistake a painter can make.

Another favorite and well-worn expression is, "It must be wonderful to have talent." This is really nothing more than a self-conscious apology. To be able to recognize talent easily is an enviable talent in itself. Most artists who are accused of having talent will accept it as flattery, but in their hearts they know it is mostly a myth. There is a man who lives in our mountain village who is a wonderful trout fisherman. He can fill a creel with trout when no one else can. He is envied by all the other fishermen and they say of him, "He's got talent—some has and some ain't." He disclaims this halo and has said, "It's because I *like* fishing and that's the way I spend most of my spare time. When you add all that time up, it makes a lot of fishing. I guess I know more about trout than they know about me."

A great deal of what this fisherman has said is true when applied to talent in painting. It is the love and interest in what you are doing that will give you an advantage, call it talent if you like. To say that anyone can paint is quite as simple as to say anyone can speak Chinese, or anyone can run a poultry farm. But to paint, just as to speak Chinese or to run a poultry farm, you must first want to and want to enough to go to some trouble; and this will not be trouble at all if you really want to. Wanting to paint is the most important asset you can have.

This desire is a tangible thing and is easily recognized by anyone from the age of two and over. Children have little difficulty in acting on this desire to paint; nothing can stop them and they should never be discouraged. We mention child art, because the amateur painter would do well to understand the courage of children. Children create in the same way as does a highly developed artist. They ignore all rules and conventions. Imagination and fantasy flow freely from their brush. There exists no subject too complicated for their will and they possess that uninhibited freedom which is a goal of every artist.

The adult beginner in painting faces two major obstacles. These are lack of

confidence and lack of technical experience. If the first obstacle is overcome, the lack of technical experience will in time take care of itself. But the reverse is not true. There are many painters who have achieved technical perfection who might be called painters without spirit. Their paintings are like pretty women without personality. What is

greatly admired is the skill the painter has exhibited; but dexterity alone is not enough. An old Chinese artist wrote:

> The spirit has no form;
> Yet, that which moves
> And transforms the form
> Is the spirit.

It is not a question of skill versus spirit because every artist wishes to do his work ably, but a less well done work should not be considered inferior if the painter has expressed himself with sincerity and courage.

A question will and should arise, why does one want to paint? Why does one choose to sit before an easel for hours, growing callouses where he shouldn't have them and messing around with sticky pigments? Why would a staid and conventional business man, while at the telephone, pick up a pencil and make strange shapes and patterns? Surely it has nothing to do with his conversation, which is probably about stocks, bonds, or carloads of produce. Why do we often find the walls of public restrooms covered with crude drawings? The question why man seems to be compelled to seek some kind of pictorial outlet is for the psychologist to answer. We recognize this need and hope this book will be an incentive to many who want to go beyond doodling.

All art expression can bring to people a new dimension of enjoyment, and a language of release from our highly mechanized world. From the amateur artist can come a real contribution to our culture, but this is possible only when the individuals bravely bring forth their most personal concepts and visions. There will be times when your painting will be laughed at, when your friends and family will be your severest critics. You should be honored by their scorn, because for centuries it has been the custom of society to be superior to its artists and then later, to be proud of them.

Someone recently asked why there should be amateur painters when we would not tolerate amateur dentists or doctors. In the practice of both of these professions there is involved the physical welfare of others. In painting, only the painter is involved, and on his canvas he may commit even the greatest atrocities and they can harm no one. The audience may complain, but it always has the privilege of not looking.

2. MATERIALS

THERE are two kinds of painters, those who buy materials to paint and those who just buy materials. The art supply store is an intriguing place, and few can resist the hundreds of gadgets that are offered. You will find easels so wonderful and so complicated that an engineer is needed to manipulate them. There will be studio lights that bend and turn in all directions, guaranteed to be superior to daylight; also stools and painting cabinets which practically work by themselves, and then,—paints of many different kinds and makes. You may ask for a tube of brown. You might as well go to a grocery store and ask for breakfast food. What *kind* of brown? The art store clerk will start listing—"burnt umber, raw umber, burnt sienna, raw sienna, alizarin, Vandyke, Verona, Mars, Spanish, sepia", etc. This same ritual can be repeated with many other colors, and for your own protection, we advise you never to go into an art store without knowing exactly what you need—and never be tempted by the glamour about you.

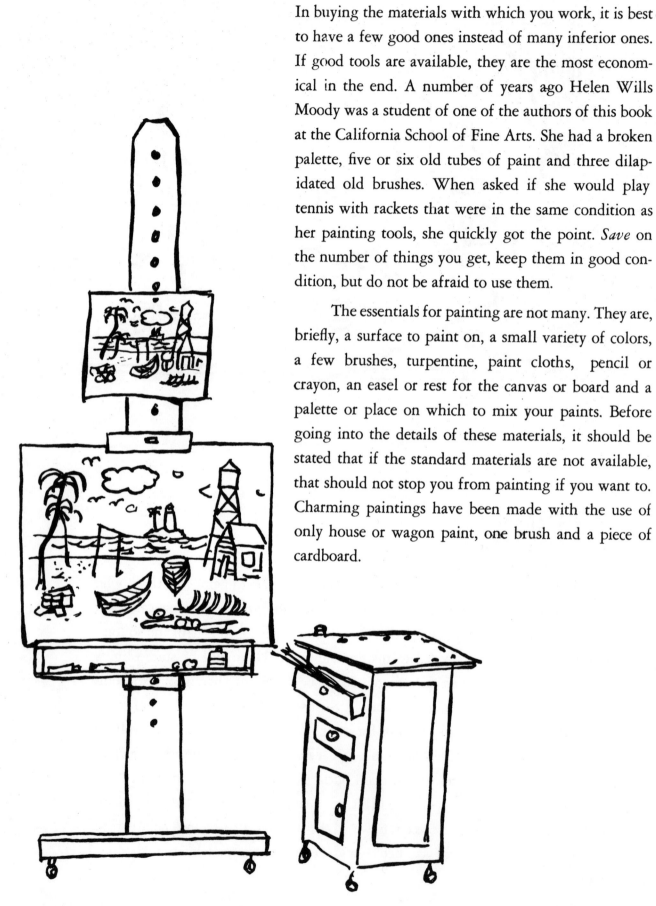

In buying the materials with which you work, it is best to have a few good ones instead of many inferior ones. If good tools are available, they are the most economical in the end. A number of years ago Helen Wills Moody was a student of one of the authors of this book at the California School of Fine Arts. She had a broken palette, five or six old tubes of paint and three dilapidated old brushes. When asked if she would play tennis with rackets that were in the same condition as her painting tools, she quickly got the point. *Save* on the number of things you get, keep them in good condition, but do not be afraid to use them.

The essentials for painting are not many. They are, briefly, a surface to paint on, a small variety of colors, a few brushes, turpentine, paint cloths, pencil or crayon, an easel or rest for the canvas or board and a palette or place on which to mix your paints. Before going into the details of these materials, it should be stated that if the standard materials are not available, that should not stop you from painting if you want to. Charming paintings have been made with the use of only house or wagon paint, one brush and a piece of cardboard.

PAINTING SURFACE

Actually, one can paint on almost anything, although most artists use a prepared canvas. You can save money and time by buying canvas in rolls of six yards or more, or on a prepared panel. The best canvas is made of linen and primed with glue and white lead pigment. The less expensive canvas is made of cotton and is adequate for a beginner. In selecting canvas we advise the choice of the finely woven

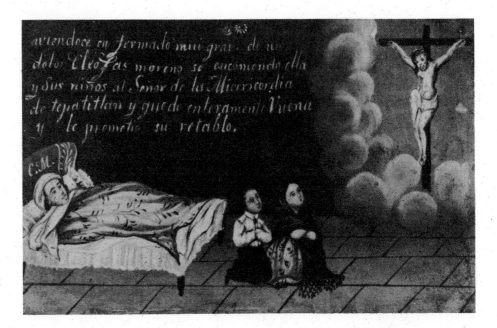

Mexican religious folk
painting on tin
Author's collection

Mexican religious folk
painting on tin
Author's collection

rather than the coarse. This canvas should have a fairly smooth surface, which will not use up great amounts of paint. Art stores also carry canvas boards (already prepared) in various sizes. These are made of cotton canvas stretched over cardboard, and are very convenient and cheap.

Any heavy paper or cardboard, first shellacked and then given a coat of white paint is a good substitute for canvas or canvas boards. Plywood, prepared in the same way can also be used. Many paintings have been done on unpolished tin or zinc sheeting.

STRETCHING OF CANVAS

If you use canvas for painting, it must be stretched on wood strips. It is best to stretch a number at a time, so that you have them on hand, and if you wish you can have them in various sizes. After you have put the wooden strips together by joining the tongue and groove corners, be sure that the stretcher is in a true square. This can be done by placing first one side, and then the other, on a level floor and tapping the opposite end with a hammer. In cutting the canvas, leave about 1 ½ inch margin beyond the size of the wood stretcher. Lay the canvas, white side down, on a table and place the stretcher on the canvas so that the margin is equal on all sides. Start tacking the canvas from the center of each side. Always stretch the canvas to the opposite side. (The tacks should be about two inches apart.) Go from one side to the other until you have reached the corners. Fold over the ends of the canvas at the corners and tack down. This can be done with less trouble if canvas pincers are used. Wooden keys come with the canvas strips and these can be forced into the corners to make the canvas tighter.

STRETCHING CANVAS

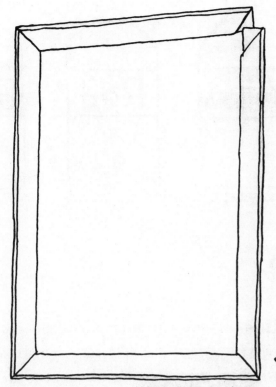

TACK CANVAS ALONG EDGE OF STRETCHER BEGINNING AT CENTER. STRETCH TO AN EVEN TENSION ON ALL SIDES. INSERT PEGS IN ALL CORNERS FOR SMOOTH PAINTING SURFACE.

STRETCHER AND PEGS

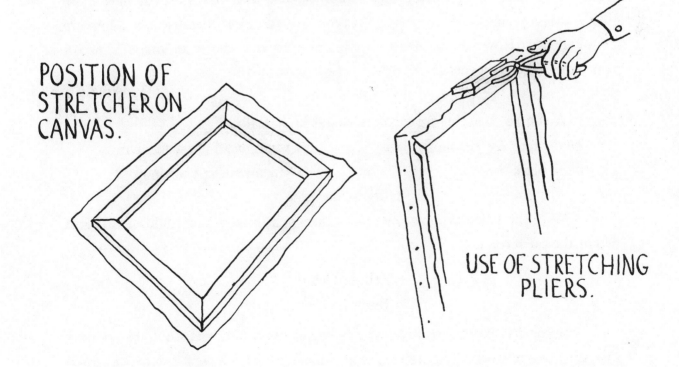

POSITION OF STRETCHER ON CANVAS.

USE OF STRETCHING PLIERS.

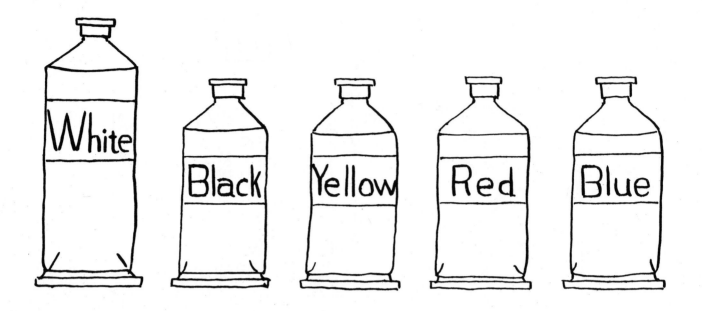

OIL PIGMENTS OR COLORS

Choosing the colors you will use becomes a trifle more difficult and every artist will have particular makes and hues he prefers. The different manufacturers of pigments do not make a standard product and may give different names to the same color. In other words, a color made by one company may have a slightly different quality or caste from that made by another. The cheaper makes usually have more filler and less pigment and, consequently, you will use more because the colors are not so intense. However, most art supply stores offer a choice of brand-name oil paints and these can generally be relied on for good quality.

A simple choice of basic colors would be as follows:

Zinc white (or titanium white)   Cadmium Yellow medium
Ivory black   Cadmium Red medium
                    Ultramarine Blue

With this palette almost any tone or hue can be mixed. You could add to these, two of the earth colors:

Yellow Ochre
Burnt Umber

If you feel more expansive, or as you gain experience and would like to have a larger choice to work from, we recommend in addition to the first palette, any or all of the following:

Cadmium Yellow light	Phthalocyanine Green
Cadmium Orange	Permanent Green light
Cadmium Red light	Viridian (green)
Indian Red	Terre Verte
Alizarin Crimson	Burnt Sienna
Cobalt Blue	Raw Umber
Phthalocyanine Blue	Mars Brown

These oil colors come in large and small size tubes. You will need twice as much white as other colors.

Many self-taught artists, having no other paint at hand, have used small cans or jars of automobile paint, furniture enamels or house paints, purchased in hardware or 5 & 10 cent stores.

ARRANGEMENT OF COLOR ON PALETTE

In arranging the paints on your palette, you should establish an order that you will become familiar with. The dark colors should be on the right going to the light ones on the left. Or, you might prefer to have white in the center and the warm colors on one side, the cool colors on the other. What is important is to choose whichever

YELLOW OCHRE   CAD.RED-M   BURNT SIENNA   BURNT UMBER   PERM. GREEN-L

TERRE VERTE

THALO GREEN

THALO BLUE

ULTRA. BLUE

IVORY BLACK

CAD. ORANGE

CAD. YELLOW-D

CAD. YELLOW-L

ZINC WHITE

order you prefer and stick to it, so that you will become as used to your color placement as a typist is to the typewriter keyboard. Keep the colors well separated in an orderly row around the top of your palette. Remember to keep the mixing area clean. When this space gets messy with splotches of paint, clean it well with a palette knife and a little turpentine on your paint cloth. If you don't do this, the messy palette soon influences whatever you are painting. When you have finished working for the day, always leave the mixing space clear, for once it dries it is hard to clean except by means of paint remover and scraping.

Do not try to paint with color that is dried up or has a heavy skin on it. One of the difficulties that hasn't been quite successfully solved, is how to keep the paint which has been squeezed from the tube from drying. If you work every day there is less waste, but if you are a weekend worker, there is bound to be considerable drying-up. This can be lessened to some extent by covering the palette, or, if you want to go to the trouble of removing each gob of paint with the palette knife and immersing it in a flat pan of water, it will stay soft without harm to the pigment.

BRUSHES

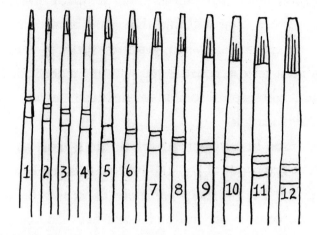

FLAT SABLE
ACTUAL SIZE

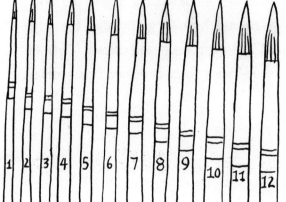

POINTED SABLE
ACTUAL SIZE

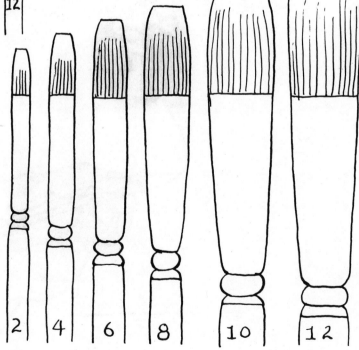

FLAT BRISTLE
ACTUAL SIZE

BRUSHES

When buying brushes it is advisable not to economize. There are many makes to select from and also many grades and sizes. You will find that good brushes are expensive, but they are your most precious tools. When you are working, they become the extension of your hand. With a little experience you will find a need and liking for certain ones. There are painters who become so fond of one brush that when it wears out they feel superstitious about replacing it.

There are two kinds of brushes used in oil painting, red or black sable and bristle. It is good to have a few of each at first, or until you know what suits you best. The sable ones are made from a fine hair. The red ones are more expensive than the black, but will last longer. The bristle brushes are made of hog's hair. The best ones are neither too sparse nor too stiff. The sizes are somewhat a matter of taste, but if you wish to be adequately supplied you should have large brushes for large areas, medium ones for smaller areas and small ones for lines and detail. The flat types are generally preferred for the larger and medium sizes, the round or pointed

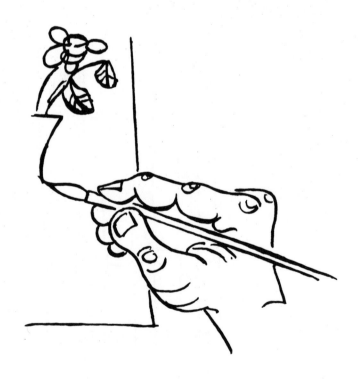

type for the small sizes. There is probably no substitute for a good brush, although at 5 and 10 cent stores or in paint shops you can sometimes pick up some that are not too bad.

Minimum requirements of brushes would be:

1 large flat bristle	1 medium flat bristle
1 medium flat sable	1 medium-small flat sable
	1 small pointed sable

Next in importance to having good brushes, is to keep them in good condition. If a brush gets sticky or filled with pigment while you are working, dip it in turpentine or a jar of kerosene and wipe it clean with your paint cloth. When you have finished work for the day, after dipping your brushes in turpentine, wash them in warm water and soap. If you should forget and let the paint harden on the brush, use paint-brush cleaner; Dic-a-doo or Oxydol are good.

PALETTE

There was a time when an artist was pictured holding a great oval-shaped palette on his arm. It was even used to symbolize his profession. But this palette, along with the velvet coat and flowing tie seems to have gone out of fashion —a very good riddance. It always seems senseless to be weighed down with this clumsy affair. Hand palettes are still used. These are the kind that come in paint boxes, but are very seldom held in the hand, usually being placed on a stool or painting table.

For indoor painting the best palette is one you can make for yourself. Obtain a piece of glass about 20 x 18 inches, then cut a piece of thick grey or white cardboard the same size. Place this under the glass and bind the edges with tape. A palette can also be made out of a smooth piece of board, which must be given several coats of varnish. After it dries, sandpaper it well.

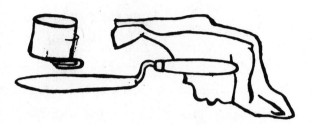

PALETTE KNIFE

When you have made a bad start and would like to remove the paint from your canvas, first scrape the color off with your palette knife. Then wash off the remaining paint with turpentine and paint cloth. The palette knife can be used in removing a part of the painting that you would like to correct or do over. Some artists use the palette knife to apply paint to the canvas. This is a little tricky and we don't especially recommend it, though there are times when it is effective.

EASEL

You will need something on which to place your canvas or painting board when you are painting. The most important thing about an easel is, that it be steady. Most art stores usually have several kinds in stock, ranging from a single outdoor sketching easel to the elaborate studio type. The sketching easel will serve two purposes: it can be used indoors as well as outdoors. It is collapsible and convenient to carry about, but, to be made stable, a weight must be attached. For anyone handy with tools, it should not be difficult to make an easel. A chair will make an excellent substitute.

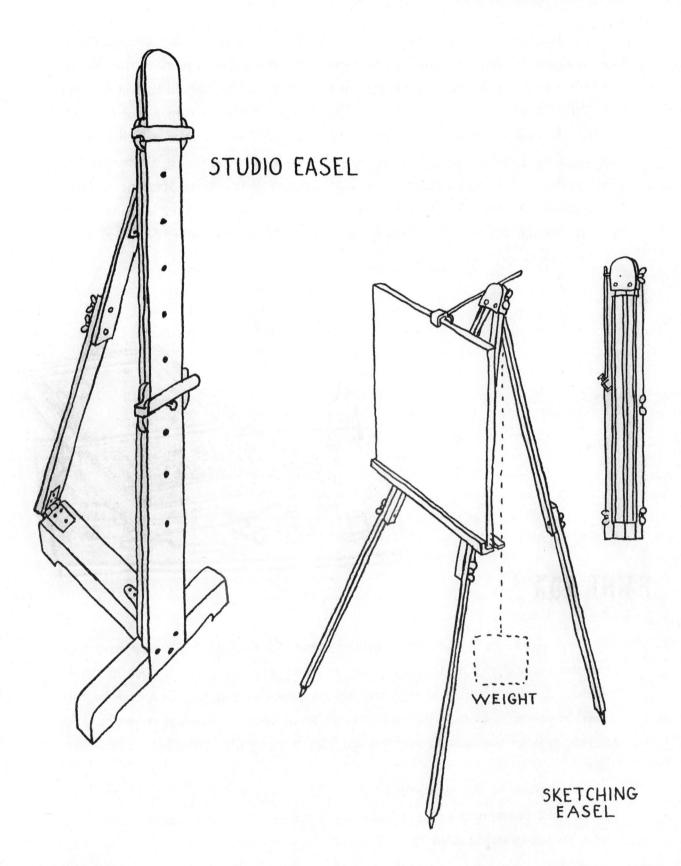

STUDIO EASEL

WEIGHT

SKETCHING EASEL

EASEL PLACEMENT

For right-handed people it is best to place the easel so that the light falls on your picture from the left. This will prevent your having to work in the shadow of your arm. If left handed, the opposite is true. Your palette should be just in front or to the side of your easel. If there is a glare of light on your picture, adjust the easel so that the canvas tips forward slightly. You may stand or sit when painting in oil, although for painting large pictures, or when you begin a picture, it is often well to look at the picture from a distance, and it is easier to do this when standing. A large piece of oil cloth placed under the easel will protect the rug or floor. Looking at the picture through a mirror placed across the room will sometimes give you a fresh view of the work in progress.

PAINT BOX

A paint box is not entirely essential, but it is convenient for one who does not paint every day. It is an orderly and protected place to keep all your materials together. A palette which fits the box always comes with it. Such boxes can be purchased in various sizes at art stores. If you are going to use the palette in the box, do not get a smaller size than 12 x 16 inches. This is especially convenient for outdoor painting.

In place of this standardized box, one can use a small fiber overnight case, sold in most department stores. Also, a metal fishing tackle box makes a good container for paints and brushes.

OLD
COSMETIC
CASE

SUPPLEMENTARY MATERIALS

MEDIUM

Oil, turpentine and damar varnish are used as a thinner when painting in oil. This is called a painting medium. Some use only the turpentine. Other commonly used mixtures are as follows:

(1) 3 drops of linseed oil
     1 teaspoon of turpentine

(2) 3 drops of linseed oil
     2 drops of damar varnish
     1 teaspoon of turpentine

(3) 4 drops of damar varnish
     1 teaspoon of turpentine

or TAUBES COPAL MEDIUM

You can mix about a half cup of medium at one time and keep it in a closed bottle.

VARNISH

— 6 MONTHS — 1 year

When the painting is finished and very dry, a retouch varnish can be thinly spread over with a large brush. This is used to bring out the color and protect the paint.

OIL CUP

This is used to hold your painting medium. It has a clasp to fasten on to the palette. Keep it covered when not in use in order to prevent the medium from evaporating and becoming thick. If it does become thick and murky, throw it away and wipe the cup clean.

SMALL MASON JAR

This is half filled with turpentine and is used to wash brushes while working.

A GOOD SUPPLY OF PAINT CLOTHS
PENCIL OR CRAYON

Most cities have art stores or stores that carry art supplies. Look them up in the classified telephone book. The following are just a few of the best-known manufacturers and distributors of art materials:

F. Weber Co., Philadelphia, Pa.

M. Grumbacher, New York, N. Y.

Winsor & Newton, Inc., New York, N. Y.

Bocour Colors, New York, N. Y.

Devoe & Raynolds Co., New York, N. Y.

Shiva Artists Colors, Chicago, Ill.

Permanent Pigments, Cincinnati, Ohio

Rembrandt Colors, Talens & Sons, Newark, N. J.

Arthur Brown & Bro., Inc., New York, N. Y.

Erwin M. Riebe Co., New York, N. Y.

Favor Ruhl & Co., New York, N. Y.

E. H. & A. C. Friedrichs & Co., New York, N. Y.

Nobema Products Corp., New York, N. Y.

Rich Art Color Co., New York, N. Y.

Sam Flax, New York, N. Y.

The companies will either send you a catalog or direct you to their nearest representatives.

3. WHAT TO PAINT

EVERYONE has fancied pictures that he would like to paint, and everyone has seen things he would like to make pictures of. There is a difference, of course, between wishing and doing. The courageous painter never hesitates because his subject seems difficult, while the timid painter will often ignore what he likes and choose a subject because he thinks it will be easy to paint. Actually, the things you would like to paint are the least difficult because there will be an interest and excitement about them. Having had some success with a particular subject, some painters will try to repeat this success. While this may give you some feeling of security, it is much better and will be more exciting to try various subjects.

Do not be too concerned about professional standards, because you will only make yourself unhappy if you reach for something for which you are not prepared. In painting, you are experiencing that rare privilege of being completely free to do or say anything you wish. You may get into technical difficulties and wish you had never taken a subject so complicated. You may feel like giving up, but don't do it. Instead, put the painting away for a few days and let it dry; then try working on it again. Perhaps

JUNGLE WITH A LION—Henri Rousseau
Museum of Modern Art

by this time your courage will have returned. Remember, in painting there are many ways of being right and each new theme you paint is your small world to do with as you wish.

Within all of us there is a great wealth of material—memories of our child-hood, events of winter and summer, of being alone, of being with many people, faces, things we like to eat, houses, trees, rooms and objects we have liked and disliked.

ANONYMOUS STILL LIFE. Colored drawing
Author's collection

Perhaps all that remains of these memories are vague sensations. For the painter these are more important than facts, because from these sensations, with the help of form and color, we make pictures.

To illustrate this process, Rousseau's "Jungle", which now hangs in the Museum of Modern Art in New York City, is an example. This painter lived in Paris most of his life, with the exception of a period of military service, when he was a

TIGER. Morris Hirshfield
Museum of Modern Art

musician in a military band. It has been pretty well established that he served in
Mexico. There he saw tropical vegetation for the first and only time in his life. Like
a true Frenchman, he saw something very exotic in this landscape. Years later, when
he painted the "Jungle", he was not making a record of the vegetation of Mexico, and
he was probably not even interested in that vegetation. What Rousseau painted were
the remembered sensations of an imaginative Frenchman in a strange land.

30

THE DREAM. Henri Rousseau
Sidney Janis collection

In creating subjects from memory, a process of elimination takes place. We seem to remember that part of an object or place which, for individual reasons, is important to us. Even something we saw yesterday is simplified and colored when it is pictured in our mind. If we should walk alone through a dark forest, and from the foliage beyond our vision would come strange sounds, we should probably feel afraid. The next day, if we were visualizing this forest, its shapes and contour would and should be influenced by that emotional experience. It is our emotional reaction that gives a painting the flavor of our particular personality. The artist who paints from his imagination has an unlimited pool of subjects to develop. The artist who paints from nature is limited to the subjects that are around him, but within this limitation many great paintings have been made. It is very helpful and stimulating, at least occasionally, to have the actual forms and colors of the subject in front of you.

There are many kinds of painting, between painting from nature and painting from one's imagination. Many times a painter will think of, or conceive a picture, and then go out and make studies from nature of material he proposes to use in his picture.

Before the day of the art school, copying of paintings was part of the tradition in the training of an artist. Today this practice is frowned upon by many teachers, although many contemporary artists will make a copy of a painting they particularly like. This is usually done as technical research. There is no reason why the self-taught artist cannot learn a great deal in this way. There are many beautifully colored reproductions made today of both past and contemporary masters. While this procedure should add to your appreciation and technical skill, we do not recommend it as a constant practice.

In selecting paintings to be reproduced in this book, we have tried to show good examples of figure, still life, portrait and landscape painting. Some of them may seem a little crude to those whose eyes have been accustomed to looking at slick magazine art and photographs. Most magazine art tries to imitate the camera. This is rather futile, for the camera can do a better job. It is a marvelous instrument, but with great limitations. It is a machine. It cannot feel, think or know. Its function is the recording on chemically coated film exactly what is in front of its mechanical glass eye. Think how limited our sense of perception would be if this were our only contact with nature!

What the human eye sees relates to all our senses. In painting a portrait of a man's head, we know the head is somewhat the shape of an egg. We know it has a back, front, top and sides. We know the flesh is warm, the cheeks are soft and the forehead hard. When we look at the face, we cannot help thinking something about the man to whom it belongs. This perception should give to the painter and his painting human values that a camera can never achieve.

The same is true for landscape. Vincent Van Gogh once said "I love to paint landscape because it is inhabited by people". You are one of those people, and you have walked over flat plains and climbed hills. You have seen the earth become warm in the spring and grow cold in the autumn. It is our feeling about a landscape that makes us want to paint it, and not its photographic appearance or its precise reflections.

Of all these subjects, still life is the most available. There are always things about the house that can be arranged on a table. Then there are the less inanimate things such as vegetables, fruits and flowers. In painting flowers, as in all other painting, there is the mass and the detail. Think out a logical painting procedure before starting. In portrait painting, remember the face is only a detail of the head. In landscape painting people, animals, buildings, trees, are the details of the fields and hills. In still life painting the table is a flat surface and on this flat surface are various shapes and these shapes have various textures.

If someone should hand you an apple, without thinking you would adjust your hand to its shape. It is this sense of shape we can use when painting. When we represent an object on canvas we give the illusion of shape, so that the eyes and senses of those who look at it are able to grasp it.

FIGURE PAINTING

One of the greatest satisfactions the artist achieves is the recording of human activity. From the time of the caveman to modern times, the artist has taken the privilege of giving man and woman great dignity. On other occasions, and with wit, he has made them and their activities seem ridiculous, as they often are. It is only the artists or art students who have become over-preoccupied with the difficulties of proportion, anatomy and likeness, who have made man seem dull and lifeless.

The authors of this book recently witnessed archaeological excavations being conducted in southern Mexico. Among the many works of art that have been found are some great stones with figure drawings scratched on their surfaces. These drawings were made by Indians about 400 B.C. It is needless to say that these Indians never had the advantage of going to art school or of reading books on how to draw with ease, yet these drawings are considered by artists, and by others with a knowledge of art, to be among the great figure drawings of all times. Unfortunately, these Indian artists left no record of their conditioning and training, but we do know that their work does not resemble photograhy and it probably never occurred to them to ask themselves if it was good or bad art. What we may learn from all figure drawing and painting is that your state of mind will be reflected in what you do. If you are afraid and think it is difficult, the figures you paint will look afraid and difficult. If you do not fear and have pleasure and excitement doing the best you can, your figures are pretty sure to express pleasure, excitement and sincerity.

Figure and portrait painting, you will find, are meat and gravy to the amateur critic, who, after indulging himself in a fit of laughter, will in a kindly and superior manner tell you what is wrong. With relish, he will say "the legs are too short" or ask "What's that thing on the face—a nose?" etc. He is having a fine time and argument with him is likely to be quite futile. The best remedy for this nuisance is to invite him to use your paints and brushes. This will sometimes change his attitude. An artist who is over-sensitive to criticism will soon become confused and discouraged.

In reality, figure and portrait painting should be less a mystery than other subjects, for most of us possess bodies and heads which have been with us long enough for us to become familiar with. Basically, human bodies are alike and differ only in small characteristics and details. When, drawing or painting from imagination, you find yourself struggling over an arm or foot, remember, you always have a model with you. With a mirror you can study any part of the body or its action. Don't stop at looking, feel the shape, because the shape will give you as much information as the appearance.

Some artists have the ability to develop in their minds complicated pictures with many figures in action and, without hesitation, they paint them. If you find yourself unable to do this, preliminary drawings or sketches may be of great assistance to you. Sometimes it is difficult to imagine a figure in a particular action. Making a simple drawing that eliminates everything but the action may help you.   (See illus.) Always remember that figure painting is not a specialty, but like any other kind of painting, it is the artist's personal interpretation that is important.

PORTRAIT PAINTING

Painting a portrait of someone usually implies that you intend to render his likeness. To do this well requires considerable skill and experience. If you haven't this skill and experience, the only way to get it is by painting portraits, and many of them. The most convenient way to go about this, is to select your most tolerant friends or relatives as subjects. Posing is a dull business and painting is the opposite; so if you want them to return and pose for you a second time, don't make them pose too long. If you should find yourself without a model, try painting a self portrait with the aid of a mirror. Rembrandt was a most prolific painter of self-portraits and each one was different from the others. He experimented with different lightings and wore many different kinds of headgear and costumes.

The composing of the picture or placing the head on the painting space should be a matter of personal choice, but by trying different arrangements you will find that some are more logical than others. If you examine many fine single figure portraits, you will find that the head is generally placed near the middle of the width of the space, although it may be high or low on the canvas. If the head is turned in the

painting, you will find it is usually turned into the greater space, and not turned to the outward side. (See Illus.) The profile of the head looking into the space seems more comfortable than the profile looking out of the space.

In placing your portrait model be sure that he or she is placed so that the light accentuates the form of the head and the essential characteristics. Sometimes a very

harsh light will cast a very dark shadow, which, if painted literally, will interfere with the likeness and completely destroy the form. It seems to us that it is far more preferable for the portrait to embody the spirit and essential character of the subject, rather than to render a slick surface likeness.

MADONNA AND CHILD. Bellini

LANDSCAPE PAINTING

NAPANOCH NEW YORK. Israel Litwak
New Art Circle

Painters of the last few generations seem to have favored landscape painting above all other subjects. Perhaps, in comparison with figure and still life painting, it is less confining. By contact or memory or both, the whole out-of-doors becomes a potential subject matter. To some it may seem easier than other subjects, although each tree and rock differs in character and shape, just as people do. It does, however, offer to many more freedom in arrangement. The timid painter has less fear of taking liberties with proportion and color, and it takes much less courage to leave out a cloud or tree than it would take to leave out an ear or a table leg. Also, landscape

seems less personal and it offers a delightful escape from all the man-made complications around us. We can listen to a farmer call in his cows and enjoy it as a part of the hills and fields; but if the man and voice were in the room with us, it would not be the same.

Landscape painting can be practised in or out of doors. Our memory storehouse of pleasant places and varied moods of nature is very full and rich. Just as a song has associations, so is a scene attached in our memory to many of the events in our lives. These scenes have been excellent subject matter for painting.

Many people feel less confident about their memory, and for them quick notes, made even from a travelling train or an automobile, can be a comforting reminder and incentive. A more definite and customary method for painting landscape indoors is first to go out and make a drawing from nature to use for the studio painting.

Painting landscape direct from nature involves a little extra trouble and tolerance. You must carry your materials to the place you select to paint and be prepared to take some of the idiosyncrasies of nature. The bugs, the mosquitoes, the wind and weather, can be disconcertingly anti-art. The changing light will probably bother the beginner more than anything else. You may select a nice shady spot and in an hour find yourself trying to paint with the sun in your eyes. A very good idea, when going out is to take two nails and a hammer instead of an easel, and find a nice tree. Nail the canvas to the tree and enjoy a healthy, shaded and comfortable afternoon of painting. The early morning and late afternoon are usually the best hours for nature sketching or painting. The overhead midday-sun glare tends to weaken the colors and neutralize the dramatic possibilities in nature. The easiest and most convenient way (if you can stand the confinement) is to paint from the back seat of your car.

Many students, when first starting to paint a landscape, will complain that there is 'too much of it' and 'they don't know what to leave out.' There IS a lot of it and one could not possibly put on a canvas everything in view. It is a matter of choice, and by selecting the things you like best you will soon find you have filled your canvas. The changing light and shadows may confuse the beginner. He may be painting a shadow on the side of a barn only to discover, an hour later, that it has disappeared.

There is no way to stop the sun moving across the sky, but you can decide where it is going to be for your painting. As you will discover, the light in nature is always changing. You may either use the change or ignore it, and become so engrossed in the enjoyment of the painting on your canvas that only approaching darkness will stop you.

THROUGH COLEMAN HOLLOW UP THE ALLEGHANY VALLEY.
John Kane
Museum of Modern Art

STILL LIFE PAINTING

In choosing objects to be used for still life painting the important thing to think of is that they (the objects) have variations in texture, color and combination of forms. It matters very little whether objects have any logical relationship. Above all, choose

things you like, even if they are not the conventional things you have seen in still life paintings. In arranging the objects, you can have almost as much fun as when you are painting. Interiors of kitchens, carpenter shops, barns, rooms, etc. make very interesting subjects.

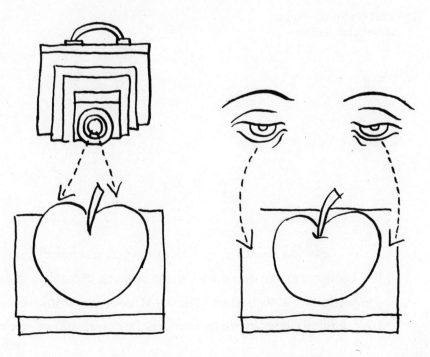

INTERIOR. Horace Pippin
Downtown Gallery

Placing paintings in the time-worn categories (such as portrait, still-life, etc.) has been a convenience only for the writers. Actually, in creative painting these categories do not always exist. The artist does not think in categories; he paints people, fruit, animals, eggs, trees, or anything he chooses in an environment he wishes.

4. PROCEDURE

IF YOU have never painted before and have purchased your colors, brushes and other material, we hope you will be so impatient to use them that you will have forgotten all about this book. After you have had some fun and calmed down a little, or, if you have painted before and are in a dilemma, you may find this chapter on procedure to be of some help.

This is a part of painting that can be taught even from a book, or by anyone who has had more experience and practice than you. Although procedure is in some ways a mechanical process, we do not say here or elsewhere that you *must* do it this way or that. We want you to examine, and, if you wish, try our suggestions. If you find them useful, they should in no way interfere with the personal elements of your painting. They should only make it easier for you to bring them out.

DRAWING AND PAINTING

Before Grandma Moses starts painting she closes her eyes until she sees a picture. She has many canvases on hand, already stretched, and they have all been given a coat of white paint. She makes a careful drawing with pencil, then she mixes a color, for instance—blue, and wherever blue is to appear on the canvas she paints it in. Then she proceeds in the same way with other colors. The details are added last. She paints with small red sable brushes, uses a table for her picture rest instead of an easel. That is Grandma Moses' way.

For those who do not see pictures when they close their eyes, there are other ways. You can think with a pencil. This method can be used by those who are painting from imagination or from nature. If you wish to paint from objects, take a pad of paper and a pencil. Look around the house until you find something that pleases you. It might be a bouquet of flowers, or a sewing basket, or vegetables on the kitchen table. Make several little drawings of these objects and, in general, an indication of the arrangement of the picture you will paint. Perhaps you will see something from the window that will be good subject matter, or perhaps you will find something you want to paint while you are out walking. Make many drawings, and from the ones you like best you start your paintings.

A great French painter once said, "Begin to paint with a broom and finish with a needle." In other words, paint the large areas first, the medium sized ones next, and the small forms last. Lines or decorations will go on easier after the paint has had time to dry a bit. A fairly definite drawing on the canvas before you start painting is a great aid.

If you work from imagination, the making of small drawings should become a habit. First, make a picture-shape and let your imagination fill it in. After you have an idea you like, draw it on your canvas, using the painting procedure suggested above. In making drawings, do not think of them as artistic creations, but rather as a pictorial shorthand. Correctness is not essential, but conviction is. When you put down a line, put it there to stay. Drawings are your personal notes; they are the outline of your thought.

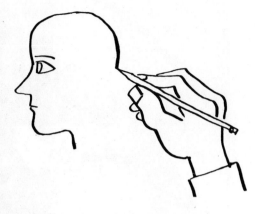

COMPOSITION AND DESIGN

As you work, you will become aware that how and where you place objects or forms within your picture space makes a great difference. It is obvious that one would not try to paint a portrait of a tall man on a picture space that is four times as wide as it was high. Almost without thinking, one would turn the canvas the other way, so that the height is greater than the width. In doing so, you are adjusting the forms of your subject to the dimensions of your canvas. This is the basis of composition.

BURIAL OF CONDE DE ORGAZ. El Greco

In all highly developed art, arrangement and design are most important factors. Our grandmothers and great grandmothers, in making quilts and hooked rugs, seemed to possess, either by knowledge or intuition, an amazing sense of design. Some housewives seem to have the ability to arrange a room so that it gives the feeling of comfort and warmth, while others, with the same materials, will make the room seem stiff and cold.

CHRIST ENTERING JERUSALEM. Giotto

In contemporary painting there is a whole school founded on design, using shapes, colors, and textures that are not representational or do not follow the forms of nature. They give enjoyment by the arrangement of these design elements within the picture space. To the amateur artist this may all seem very complicated. And so it can be.

Illustrations on pages 50 and 51 are reproductions of the work of two old masters, showing magnificent solutions of the problem of composition. The El Greco is a very complex, but beautifully ordered design. The Giotto, while simpler in organization, illustrates a fine consideration of the use of the area in which the artist painted.

There are no definite rules for making a composition, but there are a few things it is good to keep in mind when composing. For instance, if you take a given space and in it paint the head and shoulders of a woman, leaving considerable background area, you will find the woman you have painted appears to be small. Take the same space, leave very little space around the head, and you will find the woman here appears to be large.

A

B

C

You can see that even the illusion of physical appearance is governed, to some extent, by design.

At the top of this page, there are three pictures with lines drawn across them. These lines represent the skyline. In Illus. A there is a feeling of largeness and space. In Illus. B, a more intimate feeling, and in Illus. C there is a lesser amount of both these qualities.

Another example (right) is where you have a number of forms or objects intersecting the boundaries of the picture space. The picture will not look complete in itself, but will seem like a piece cut from another picture.

It is well to remember that the surface you work on is more than just a place to put a painting. The consideration of its dimensions can be of great help to you. When a story is well composed, it is easy to read and understand. When a painting is well composed, it is easy to see and enjoy.

VALUES

In the use of color, there is an element which is of great importance: the quantity of light and dark each color possesses. This is called value. Values can be more clearly defined when colors are reduced to blacks, grays and white. Forms are made recognizable by how they are affected by light and shade. Look at the reproductions in this book and notice that there are thoughtful variations of values involved. You will notice how well defined and clear these pictures are. It is because these artists made use of values by composing them well, by keeping spaces simple in value,

QUAI D'AUTEIL.
Henri Rousseau
Collection Max Weber

RIVER SCENE.
Henri Rousseau
Collection Max Weber

and by bringing out objects with contrasting values. Painters in the past often first made black and white value drawings to aid them in the final color construction. The color that is the lightest is yellow and the darkest, violet. Red, green and blue have intermediate values.

COLOR

The color on your palette is to you what the keyboard of a piano is to a composer. You, also, are a composer, but instead of composing for the ear, you compose for the eye. There are physical laws governing the reaction of the eye to the waves of reflected light, which cause one color to be different from another. This concerns the artist indirectly. What really concerns the artist is to make color do what you want it to. It is color more than anything else that makes your canvas lively or dull. It possesses infinite qualities that the painter uses; it can be masculine or feminine, shrill or soft, harsh or mellow, sombre or gay, hot or cold and so on, until we have touched upon everything that affects the senses.

The reader may not be familiar with some of the terms we are using. In mentioning warm and cool colors, we mean that colors we use on our palette can, more or less, be divided into two categories. The reds, oranges and yellows are generally considered warm colors; green, blue and violet, cool colors.

Following is the division of your palette colors:

WARM

Cadmium yellow medium
Cadmium yellow dark
Cadmium Orange
Cadmium Reds
Yellow Ochre

Burnt Umber
Indian Red
Raw Umber
Mars Brown
Burnt Sienna

Alizarin

COOL

Cobalt Blue
Ultramarine Blue
Thalo Blue
Thalo Green
Viridian Green
Permanent Green light
Terre Verte

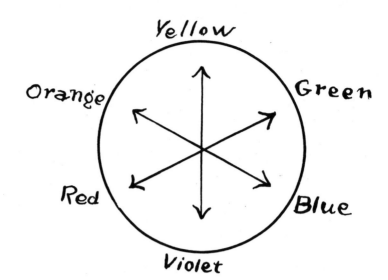

Black and white are generally cooling to colors. Both alizarin and Indian red, although in the warm category, when mixed with white become distinctly cool reds.

In a painting, the warm colors project themselves (they are also called "advancing" colors) and the cool colors recede. The colors that predominate in the world we live in are a mixture of warm and cool. In the winter, or on the ocean, cool is dominant.

In the spring we have warm colors, and some cool; in the summer, cool with some warmth; and in the autumn, warm is dominant. If you look at a crowd of people on the street or at a ball game, you will notice the intermingling of warm and cool. In the room you are now in, you will find the same intermingling. All this may seem irrelevant to painting, but this is not true. What we have been doing is to examine the colors of nature and the nature of color. When the artist creates he does not copy nature; he uses it for his pleasure and desires.

Complementary colors complement or oppose each other. Above is a simple chart of these color extremes. A complementary color has the faculty of making the other color seem more intense. If you paint a green apple on a background that has an amount of red in it, the green apple will seem more brilliant than if painted on a blue or yellow background.

To show further the influence of one color upon another, paint a grey form on a green background and it will seem to be a warm grey or have red in it. If the grey form is painted on a red background, it will seem to be cool or have some green in it. As we can change the physical appearance of shapes by arrangement and design, so can we change the appearance of color by the surrounding color.

Canvas usually comes in a whitish color, and using this white to paint on has, without doubt, an influence on your scheme of colors. In painting colors on the white, you use those that please you in relation to the white ground. To give the canvas a reddish tone, you would automatically use colors related to the reddish tone. It is good at times to vary the canvas tone with a thin turpentine color wash before you start painting.

Many books have been written on color theories. Aside from the simple facts above, we do not think you will be greatly aided by further complicated theoretic study. Most painters and paintings violate everything the theorist has said. Colors and color combinations we like are very important personally and are intuitive choices.

TEXTURE

Use of different textures when painting is very exciting and has a very rewarding result. All things we see have different textures: the sky is usually smooth, tree

SKATING ON LAKE CARASALJO. Israel Litwak
New Art Circle

BRINGING IN THE MAPLE SUGAR. Grandma Moses
Galerie St. Etienne and British American Art Centre

foliage is speckled and the bark is rough. Materials differ greatly in texture, from shiny, smooth satin to printed calico. Water doesn't feel like glass and, although it may be the same color, it doesn't look like it either.

It is a very good exercise

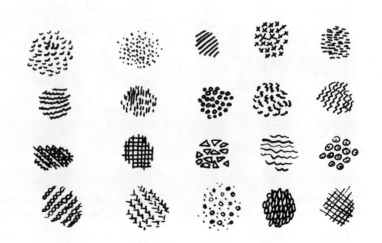

THE OLD APPLE TREE. Frederick Papsdorf
Perls Gallery

to try to limit the color in a picture and to heighten all the textures. You will find that, besides your palette of color, an invented palette of textures is possible. You can use all-over patterns (as in rugs) strips, dots, checks, thin or thick paint, different

61

WASHINGTON UNDER THE COUNCIL
TREE. Joseph Pickett
Newark Museum

brush strokes, and many other varieties that the subject will suggest to you.

You may use the different textures realistically, or you may use them simply because you enjoy them and want them in your design.

PERSPECTIVE

Perspective, as it has been taught, is a maze, and once you enter it, it becomes almost impossible to find your way out. We shall not take you into the maze, but shall try to look at it from the outside. Painting and drawing are illusions insofar as they attempt to represent depth on a flat surface. One of the means of doing this is perspective.

There are complicated laws of perspective but they are within the maze and we shan't touch them. We shall use only the eye. For example, if you are on the ground looking up at an eight story building, how would the top of the building appear in comparison with a view of the same building from the top of another building twice as high? Illus. E gives the illusion of looking up. Illus. F, of looking down. Illus. G is where no perspective was used. In painting such a building there may be times when you want the building to appear flat as buildings sometimes do. Then you would ignore perspective (as in Illus. G). The other two diagrams give the building volume and height.

E

F

G

True perspective is seldom used by the artist; but to know it often gives one more confidence in violating it. Most dictionaries and encyclopedias will give you simple basic rules. Simplest and most easy to understand is that all parallel lines converge to a horizon line, which is the eye-level. You have noticed this, no doubt, when you have looked down an avenue or a railroad track. Illus. H.

H

I

J

Perspective is often used when drawing the human figure. This is called fore-shortening and becomes difficult when you are only following the outlines of the figure,—not thinking of it as a shape. Illus. I shows an arm resting on a table. Illus. J shows the same arm thought of in perspective. Illus. K shows a head looking up, with perspective lines similar to the building in Illus. E. Illus. L shows the head looking down and corresponds in perspective to the building in Illus. F.

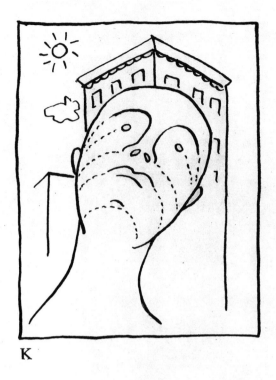

K

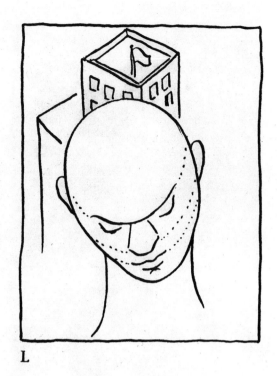

L

M

N

Diminishing the size of receding objects will give the sensation of space or distance. Illus. M shows a landscape. Illus. N shows the same landscape, giving space illusion by diminishing sizes.

BUSY STREETS. Philip Pieck
Contemporary Arts

THE STATUES AT FORT MARION. A. M. Vedovelli
Perls Gallery

LANDSCAPE. Henri Rousseau
Metropolitan Museum

The ancient Chinese artists used the reverse of our perspective, in order to bring the objects farther away into prominence. This compensates for the natural importance of the foreground, thus aiding the artists in the distribution of interest throughout his picture.

What we have said in this chapter on perspective may be used as a clue for the beginner. It may be of interest to you to study this further, but do not let perspective, when your are painting, enslave you.

5. PROCEDURE ON TWO PICTURES BY DORIS LEE

I chose these two pictures because they were done in simple, clear stages. It is the way I usually paint, unless I am experimenting, which often happens.

"THE SLEIGH"

Figure A is a photograph from a page in my sketch book. It is about 4¼ by 6 inches in actual measurement. I did not draw it from nature. I was just sitting and thinking

THE SLEIGH. Doris Lee. (A)

THE SLEIGH. Doris Lee. (B)

about Winter, and those were the things that came to my mind. I had seen an old sleigh in a farmyard nearby a while ago.

I measured the general proportions of the little sketch and stretched a canvas 24 x 32 inches.

Figure B shows a rough drawing on the canvas. I didn't bother to draw in any of the details, because I knew I would paint the larger masses first. I merely wanted an indication of the main shapes. Then I rubbed a yellowish warm tone over the whole canvas, because I intended to paint the snow

THE SLEIGH. Doris Lee. (C)

white and did not want to be bored painting white on white.

Figure C shows the first stage of painting. The sky was put in first and it was pretty well finished before anything else was painted. I made the sky a warm gray, because the snow would be a cold color. The objects in the snow scene would be warmer in color and have a relation to the sky. Next the distant hills were painted in flatly and then the foreground and some of the larger objects. I had the sleigh painted in earlier, but did not like it and painted it out with white paint. I decided to wait until it had dried before painting in another sleigh.

Figure D is the finished painting. Again I put in the sleigh, which went on easily over the dry white paint. Then the trees were developed, some texture and shape put in the snow and the house and barn completed. Last, I finished the woman and horses and, finally, the chickens, the owls and twigs. After the picture had dried and I had varnished it, a few color and accent corrections were made.

THE SLEIGH. Doris Lee. (D)

"MAYPOLE"

This picture, also, was started from a little sketch in my note book. I had always remembered the Maypole Dance and the colored streamers swinging around and weaving against the sky, as a very pretty sight. It has always been to me a fine symbol of Spring.

MAYPOLE. Doris Lee. (E)

Figure E shows the first rough sketch on the canvas. While the drawing is crude, I try to make it very definite and in pleasing proportions, as the main compositional areas in the canvas. That is, the division of sky and land, the shapes not only of the school and trees, but also of the spaces between objects in the picture, which we call negative areas as opposed to positive areas. Many times I draw shapes I like and then let them represent whatever they may turn out to be.

MAYPOLE. Doris Lee. (F)

I was once told by an art teacher not to call attention to the exact centre of the canvas. For me, this was bad advice, for I have found the centre of the canvas to be very important. In this case, I made sure the maypole was exactly there. The clouds were so placed as to relate to the pole and to help decorate it. I did not want the sky to look like a section of a sky. I wanted it to be *the* sky for this picture.

Figure F shows the first painting stage. After I blew fixative over my drawing

MAYPOLE. Dors Lee. (G)

I washed warm and cool colors over the whole surface of the canvas. Then I painted in the sky with thin pigment. I knew that I would repaint it later, and wanted to have a hint of the bright colors underneath the gray of the sky. Next, I spotted colors all over the foreground. It is necessary to make decisions in color that cannot be made in drawing or outline and, when painting, very often changes are made from the original drawing.

In this reproduction (Fig. F), I noticed that two dogs were indicated. This reminds me of a story once told about the American painter, Albert Ryder. A man was admiring a landscape of his in which there was an angel by a rock. "You know," he said to Ryder, "the composition is beautiful and the angel is in just the right place." Ryder turned and said, "She ought to be. I've had her all over the lower half of the canvas."

And so with my dogs. I hope they have at last landed in the right place.
Figure G is the finished picture.

6. THE SELF TAUGHT PAINTER

All painters are to some degree self taught, but many have had the experience of an apprenticeship or several years in art school, which has given them at least some technical facility. Most artists, through their own efforts or through some financial aid, devote all their time to painting. The true self-taught painter usually has had, or has, some other occupation and does not think of painting as a profession. Rather, it is something he likes to do to the extent of giving it most of his spare time.

Within the professions of medicine, dentistry and law, there are many amateur artists. In New York City there have been frequent exhibitions of paintings by doctors. During the war, and now, under the auspices of seamen's welfare organizations, merchant seamen painted many pictures of their wartime experiences. Much of this work was done at sea. In many other trades there are numberless individuals who paint for relaxation and enjoyment. In practically all instances these professional men and workers in the different trades are finding their own way into a wholesome and gratifying personal experience.

The examples of paintings reproduced here were, for the most part, done by people whose primary reason for painting was for pleasure. Through this kind of expression art had its beginnings and the self-taught artists have always been a factor in the growth of art. They have been called

From a Young Woman's Sketch Book.
   Mid 19th Century. Sketch 1
   Courtesy F. A. R. Galleries

From a Young Woman's Sketch Book.
Mid 19th Century. Sketch 2
Courtesy F. A. R. Galleries

by various names—primitive, naive, artists of the people, folk artists, amateur artists, etc. Regardless of what they are called, they are the foundation of our pictorial heritage and culture. They have enriched us and can continue to give some human visions of life that the trained artist sometimes considers unimportant.

Of the early American work reproduced in this book, there is little known of the artists as individuals. What is known is that in the Eastern States in the late 18th and 19th centuries the amateur painter was not uncommon. It was as customary for young ladies to paint, in this period, as it was for them to play the piano a few generations later. The seminaries gave them encouragement. Many of their paintings were in water color or in oil on velvet. Also, there were many sign-and-coach painters who took to making pictures. Out of these trades came the travelling portrait painter, who, like the Fuller Brush man, went from house to house. Some of these painters became highly skilled at their trade, others less so. Many of the paintings that have survived are now in museums and in private art collections, not as relics of the past, but because they are things of beauty.

About the most famous of the self-taught artists is Henri Rousseau. He was born in France in 1844 and began to paint at about the age of 35. He had tried many occupations, the last as customs inspector in the outskirts of Paris. Later, when retired on his small government pension, he gave music lessons and thus had more time for his painting. His wife, who ran a small stationery store, displayed his pictures, priced at a few dollars, in the window. Today these same pictures sell for many thousands of

From a Young Woman's Sketch Book.
Mid 19th Century. Sketch 2
Courtesy F. A. R. Galleries

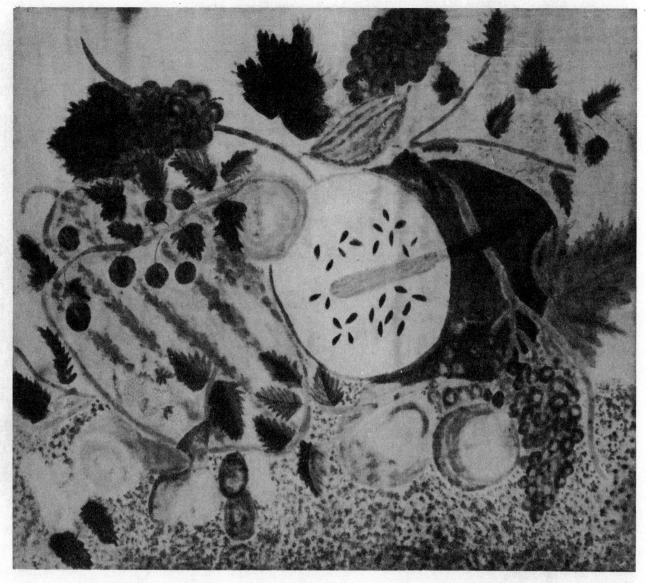

dollars. Rousseau was "discovered" by a number of French artists. Before he died in 1910 he had become a very famous man and his pictures now hang in many museums throughout the world.

Camille Bombois is also a well-known French primitive. At the age of sixteen, while working as a farm helper, he began making drawings. As a young man he was a wrestler and circus performer. Later, in Paris, he worked nights as a laborer and in this way had a few hours of daylight that he could use for painting. He was a powerfully built man and in the first World War won many decorations for his reckless bravery.

AGNES FRAZEE AND BABY. Anonymous
Downtown Gallery

Louis Vivin, another Frenchman, worked a good part of his life as a postal inspector, but he always managed to find time to paint. He died in Paris at the age of 78.

Of the American self-taught artists, Pickens and Hicks are the old masters. Edward Hicks was born in Bucks County, Pennsylvania, in 1780. At the age of 13 he was apprenticed to a coach maker. Besides learning to build coaches, he learned to paint them, thereby also learning the grinding of colors and making of brushes. After his apprenticeship he went into business for himself, painting signs, houses and por-

SIGN Painted by H. E. Covill 1886
N. Y. Historical Society

traits. He then became a preacher, dividing his time between painting houses and pictures, preaching and doing a little farming on the side. Amusingly enough, he wrote, "Painting appears to me to be one of those trifling, insignificant arts, which has never been of any substantial advantage to mankind. But as the inseparable companion of voluptuousness and pride, it has presaged the downfall of empires and kingdoms, and in my view stands now enrolled among the premonitory symptoms of the rapid

POET'S BOUQUET. Henri Rousseau
Museum of Modern Art

BEFORE ENTERING THE RING. Camille Bombois
Museum of Modern Art

decline of the American Republic." Such drastic comment was probably recorded on a day when his painting went badly. He continued to paint until the day before his death. More than anything else, Hicks loved to paint animals, and though the titles of his paintings were "The Grave of William Penn", "The Residence of David Twinging", and the "Peaceable Kingdom", the animals were always prominent.

Joseph Pickett spent all of his life in New Hope, Pennsylvania, and was the proprietor of a country grocery store. Up to this time, only three of his pictures have been discovered. After his death these paintings brought only a dollar each at a local auction. Today they could probably not be purchased at any price.

CHURCH OF ST. LAURENT AND THE GARE DE L'EST
Louis Vivin
Museum of Modern Art

Horace Pippin was a Negro. He was entirely self-taught and greatly respected by his fellow artists. His work hangs in many museums and private collections. Pippin was born in 1888. Although always interested, he did not start painting until 1930. He left school at the age of 15 and worked for several years as a porter. He was badly wounded in the first World War and many of his subjects for painting are from his memories of the war. His method of painting was to think over what he was going to paint until all of its details are pictured in his mind. He used few colors and did not hesitate to give a painting all the time it needed. He felt that it is impossible for one to teach another about art and that the greatest advantage one can have is a love of it.

John Kane, whose paintings have been very much sought after by collectors, died in Pittsburgh in 1934. He was born in Scotland in 1860, coming to America when he was 19 years old. He worked as a laborer and later took up the trade of house painting. Although he had always wanted to be an artist, he didn't begin to paint until he was 60. His subjects were mostly factory scenes painted from a window of the tenement where he lived. When asked why he liked to paint, he said "I love puttin' on the color."

THE PEACEABLE KINGDOM. Edward Hicks
Museum of Modern Art

Vincent Canade went to art school for one day. His work is now in the collections of the Phillips Memorial Museum in Washington, the Newark Museum, Whitney Museum and the Museum of Modern Art. He worked as a house painter for many years, painting his pictures in his spare time.

Lawrence Lebduska, born in Maryland in 1894, was taken to Europe, where he was trained as a stained-glass window

CORYELL'S FERRY. Joseph Pickett
The Whitney Museum

artisan. Since returning to this country he has worked at this trade and at painting. His pictures are in many collections.

Vedovelli, now 77 years old, was born in Italy but has lived in this country for over 50 years. The last twenty were spent in St. Augustine, Florida, where he has worked as a caretaker and gardener. He began to paint about eleven years ago. His subjects for the most part are the streets, buildings

THE HOLY MOUNTAIN. Horace Pippin
Downtown Gallery

PANTHER HOLLOW. John Kane
The Whitney Museum

and monuments around St. Augustine. His paintings were first discovered hanging on the walls of a drug store. They were for sale, priced at a few dollars. He had his first exhibition in New York in 1945.

Raisa Robbins was born in Russia. Before coming to this country in 1922, she was a pianist. She started painting after an illness, about six years ago. She paints entirely from memory. Many of her subjects are scenes from her childhood and, like most other self-taught artists, she first pictures the arrangement and details of her paintings in her mind. If the subject is complicated, she will make a pencil drawing before painting. Her paintings all seem to have the cheerfulness which is characteristic of peasant art.

SELF-PORTRAIT. Vincent Canade   *Weyhe Gallery*

Father Pieck was born in Holland in 1881 and started painting while studying for the priesthood in London. This self-taught artist spent 32 years as a missionary in the Philippines. Instead of painting the exotic tropical subjects about him for so many years, his paintings are gray, somber memories of Holland. Father Pieck has had three exhibitions in New York and, recently, one in Brazil.

Mickey Walker, the world's former welter-weight and middleweight champion, forty years old and unschooled in art, began to paint as an avocation. His artistic career began simply because Mickey thought it would be fun to paint. He is now determined to become a great artist. He had his first one-man show at the ACA Gallery in New York in November, 1945.

Israel Litwak is now 78 years old. He started painting in 1935. He was a cabinet maker, but because of his age he found it difficult to obtain work at his trade. Being a normally active man, he wanted to keep his hands at work, and started painting. He says, "I work from memory of the times I used to travel around." His work is exhibited at the New Art Circle in New York.

Frederick Papsdorf was born in 1887, the son of a minister of an Ohio country church. He recognized early in life his love and talent for sketching, but did not attempt to paint in oil until 1934. Since then, he has sold over 250 paintings to museums and private collectors, among them, the Detroit Institute of Art, Museum of Modern Art, Whitney Museum, Charles Laughton and Greta Garbo. Mr. Papsdorf lives in Detroit, where for many years he has been employed by a milk company checking bottles. He devotes Sundays and after-working hours to his painting. Through the courtesy of Mr. Papsdorf and the Perls Galleries, we quote from some biographical notes written by Mr. Papsdorf, which we feel are typical of the development of a self-taught artist:

"The urge to paint made itself felt very early in my life. Copying small landscapes, houses, trees, birds, then coloring them with crayon or water color; a few have survived the years of wear and tear. A little later, ten cent tubes of color were bought from the mail order house, pictures were produced on linen, cardboard, or whatever

THE LIGHTHOUSE. Antonio Vedonelli
Perls Gallery

materials were available, as money was scarce, and there
were no schools available for instruction. I had to rely on
my father for help, who bought illustrative books covering
the various subjects such as figures, animals, houses, flowers
and small landscapes. Out of this group of oils, a few also
survive. The surprising fact is, where no ground prepara-
tions were made, and a cheap color used, the color remained
surprisingly well.

"Having attained the age where it was necessary to work, various jobs were tried, in the evenings and Sundays; spare time was filled in by drawing, some water color, and pen work. A correspondence course had a good start, but was later abandoned for a trip to the South, where more sketches were produced. In the long winter evenings,

RUSSIAN EASTER TABLE. Raisa Robbins
Durand-Ruel

SKATERS. Philip Pieck
Contemporary Arts

when not going out to see the girl of my choice, I spent the time drawing, and also doing some wood carving, consisting of Indian heads. All were given away, but one has survived, which today adorns my pipe rack. After my marriage, the Sunday afternoons and some nights were spent sketching and also doing some water color work.

"About 1928, I secured a job in a creamery, where I was assigned to the job of checking cases. Because it was monotonous, I encountered a little sketching.

"In the Spring of 1932 I enrolled in the Friday evening sketch class of the Detroit Institute of Arts.

"Oil painting was now my goal. Canvas was bought, oil colors were purchased here and there, and the start was made in 1934.

"Original sketches were made while driv-

99

METROPOLITAN OPERA HOUSE. Israel Litwak
New Art Circle

ing through the country side. Flowers and weeds were gathered for material, but I did not know much about the preparation of canvas, or what color to use. Upon approaching Sarkis for lessons in oil, he again told me, 'You are doing well, and need no lessons'. Pictures then were developed at a haphazard manner. Eventually through conversation and books, I enriched my knowledge, having originally used turpentine as a medium. I now switched to the ordinary linseed oil which was an improvement over turpentine, and then a better set of oils was secured. A set of Grumbacher's Pre-Test oils was also an improvement over my oddly assorted collection of oils.

ASTERS. Fred Papsdorf
Perls Gallery

"I bought a book by Bertram Nicholls which was a great aid to me. I began to use a good grade of linen for my oils, and also switched to Schmincke Finest, Grumbacher's best grade of oils, and also sun-thickened linseed oil as a medium.

"In 1938 when the Museum of Modern Art held its Realists and Magic Realism Show, ten of my oils were included. Mr. Perls, viewing the show and seeing my work, wrote me a letter, and I quote: 'And it occurred to me possibly you would like a dealer and a show in New York.' That letter was like manna from heaven.

"The time was now moving swiftly to the date of my first 'one man show' in New York. Having arrived in New York the night previous to the show, I was immediately taken to

the gallery. To see one's own pictures so artistically framed and hung in a well lighted gallery in that great city, was, to say the least, 'a real thrill'. To be interviewed and have your picture taken as well as articles written in the local newspapers and magazines is something you do not forget quickly.

"A second 'one man show' followed in September, 1945, which also was a success.

"The last improvement made at this time was a studio, for I had previously used a corner of the dining room. This change gave me the advantage of a flexible easel, a cabinet to store my painting equipment, as well as an arrangement whereby the articles of a still life could be lighted to my advantage."

THE HENRY SWISHER FARM
Painted by H. O. Kelly, a farm worker in Blanket, Texas
Collection Gill Kornblee

The work of Grandma Moses is covered elsewhere in this book. There are many, many more self-taught artists, and many yet to be discovered. If you are an amateur painter, after reading this chapter you may think that you, too, may become

FRUIT STILL LIFE. Anonymous
Courtesy of Betty Barnes

famous and sell many pictures. You may, but you must remember that to become famous and sell pictures was not the reason these people painted. They enjoyed painting, and the fame was an incidental by-product.

Painted by A. G. Carter, who is a cobbler in Appalachia, Virginia.
Collection Lucile Blanch

Colored drawing by Vedovelli, of St. Augustine, Florida.
From Collection of the Author

7. APPRECIATION

Painting for enjoyment probably depends very little on your appreciation of other painters' work. Many painters are so intensely involved in their own painting that they have little interest in the work of others. There will be some who are not this way, and for these there is no reason why the liking of pictures painted by others should not be an added enjoyment and stimulation. It is not our intention to tell you what pictures to like, but we wish to help you like many.

In our democracy we are proud of our rights as individuals, but we do very little to practice those rights. When a high school girl goes to school wearing flowers

IMAGINATIVE PICTURE BY EDWARD HICKS.
Valentine Dudensing Gallery

WINTER QUIET. Patsy Santos
Whitney Museum

on her shoes, she will either be ridiculed or 20,000 other high school girls will copy
her. Unfortunately, in the appreciation of art the same sort of thing has taken place.
In painting, there should be as many interpretations as there are individuals painting,

FOR ABRAHAM LINCOLN—THE GREAT
EMANCIPATOR. Horace Pippin
Downtown Gallery

because, basically, painting is the product of the individual. It is one of the few occupations left in the world where the individual functions alone. If there are many different kinds of people making pictures, the results should be many different kinds of painting. In the appreciation of painting, the painter should be the first to accept this fact.

If you were to look in the museums in Europe and in this country you would

RUNAWAY HORSE. Anonymous
Whitney Museum

begin to understand the infinite range of art. For one person to appreciate it all is impossible, but if the mind is not closed, a true appreciation of painting can bring to you the entire "history of a man's imagination" and his visual pleasures.

GRACE'S ANTIQUE SHOP. Raisa Robbins
Durand-Ruel

LANDSCAPE WITH HOUSES.
Grandma Moses
Galerie St. Etienne and British-American Art Centre

GENERAL MARION FEASTING THE BRITISH
OFFICER ON SWEET POTATOES. G. W. Mark
N. Y. Historical Society

Seeing in painting all the qualities of each individual artist's intention and expression, is the basis of appreciation. The self-taught painter may find it difficult to find anything he likes in some of the paintings being made today. He may think it is

NIGHT IN THE JUNGLE. Lawrence Lebduska.
Contemporary Arts

wrong for the artist to stray so far from nature. It is true that many modern painters have either abstracted from nature only a few fundamental forms, or have completely disregarded the conventional physical appearance of natural forms. These artists are using the freedom that is every artist's right, to express his concepts in new and invented forms.

Truly creative painting, in any mood or form, is part of the unchanging desire of man to express himself. There may be prejudice and disagreement and active dislike aroused by painting, as well as entirely agreeable reactions. This proves that painting is dynamic and an active factor in shaping many of our living patterns. Through direct participation in art, and with some familiarity with its history, it is not difficult to realise why its forms are always changing, and that to have many kinds of painting is to have many kinds of enjoyment.

A few summers ago, some ladies in a small Eastern town decided that they should have an art exhibition. One of the ladies offered an idea. Instead of having as usually artists vacationing in the vicinity offer their work, the decision was to promote an exhibition of work by natives of the town. The fact that there were no native artists did not bother the lady in the least. Painting kits were assembled and distributed throughout the town. The plumber got one; so did the carpenter, the garageman, the house painter and many others. A prize was offered for the best painting. Before long most residents of the town were painting, and still are painting.

These people added to their lives a new realm of

enjoyment and it is one that they can continue to enjoy throughout their lives. This can be done in other towns and villages, and there is no doubt that it will be done. It will take a little initiative on someone's part, but almost every small town has such leaders.

For many years, painting has been recognized by physicians and psychiatrists as having a therapeutic value. People who have been ill or have had nervous disorders can, by becoming interested in painting, forget their troubles and thus aid themselves to recovery. All the arts are being increasingly used in military and veterans' hospitals to help the men forget the horrors of war. The authors do not offer painting as a cure for everything, but what we do offer is our belief that participation in art is a robust and lively activity, of direct value to all people. For the amateur in art it is well to discard all ideas that painting is reserved for special people. As a personal practice, participation in art and artists' activities should be as obvious and understandable as participation in a baseball game.

8. OTHER PAINTING MEDIA

WATER COLOR

Both water color and gouache are effective media for painting. Watercolor, although more commonly used, is probably more difficult to handle and is almost impossible to fumble with as a medium. Much of its charm is in its freshness, transparency and directness. To make changes is not easy and tends to destroy its effectiveness. Therefore, the artist who uses it well must have skill.

Compared with oil painting, water color is less expensive and more convenient to handle. A set of colors can be purchased for 50 cents or more, depending on the quality. Brushes come in many different qualities. The best are red sable. They are round and should taper to a fine point. For washing in larger areas of color, it is well to have some larger flat sable brushes. The best painting surface is called water color paper, obtainable in different grades, weights and textures. The paper is first made wet and then the edges are tacked or pasted to a drawing board. As it dries, it becomes a tight, smooth surface. Some artists prefer to paint on it before it has dried; others wait until it has dried. After a brief drawing is made on the paper, the large areas are washed in, then the details.

GOUACHE

Gouache is opaque water color. It comes in tubes or jars and is sold under various trade names, such as Show-Card colors, tempera, casein tempera, etc. Almost any cardboard makes a suitable surface to paint on. Many artists who work in this medium prefer illustration board. Gouache, unlike water color, will take quite a bit of fumbling or working over, and makes it a good medium for the beginner. After cutting the cardboard to the size desired, it should be thumb-tacked to a drawing board to prevent warping. The sequence of developing a picture is the same as in oil painting, the difference being that gouache dries in a few minutes. This allows the artists to work over the surface without the color underneath interfering. Either water color or oil brushes, or both, may be used. Gouache dries flat and slightly lighter than when first applied. It may be framed like either a water color or an oil painting.

GENERAL ADVICE

GESSO PANELS

Gesso (pronounced jess-o) has become more and more a favored surface to paint on by artists. It is a mixture of glue and whiting applied to a surface. Masonite is a very good material to use. A good gesso is difficult to mix, and it is recommended that a prepared gesso be bought at the art store and that the directions on the box be followed. A good brand is made by Permanent Pigments. A teaspoon of linseed oil added slowly, while stirring, to each quart of gesso, will keep it from cracking and from being too absorbent.   *or* WHITE (FLAT) LATEX [EXTERIOR — INTERIOR]

VARNISHING A PAINTING

There are two ways of varnishing a painting. If the paint is not thoroughly dry, a retouch varnish can be carefully blown on with an atomizer. If dry, the varnish can be thinly laid on with a soft flat brush about an inch wide. It is best to have the canvas slightly warm before varnishing. Also, as far as possible, do your varnishing in a dust-free atmosphere. Tip the canvas toward the light to make sure you have not missed parts of the surface.

ARTIFICIAL LIGHT

If one wishes to paint at night or in a poorly lighted room, the fluorescent lights now being sold make an excellent substitute for daylight.

PORTRAIT PAINTING

A mirror behind you, adjusted so that your sitter can watch you paint, will interest him and help him to keep his pose. This is especially good when painting children.

If you paint the general shapes, colors and textures, you will find that the likeness will take care of itself.

FRAMES

The simplest way to solve the framing problem is to buy raw wood frames. Give them several coats of flat white paint. After drying, they can be toned by rubbing on floor wax, to which has been added a very small amount of raw umber or black. If you get the tone too dark, you can wipe it off with a cloth and a little turpentine.

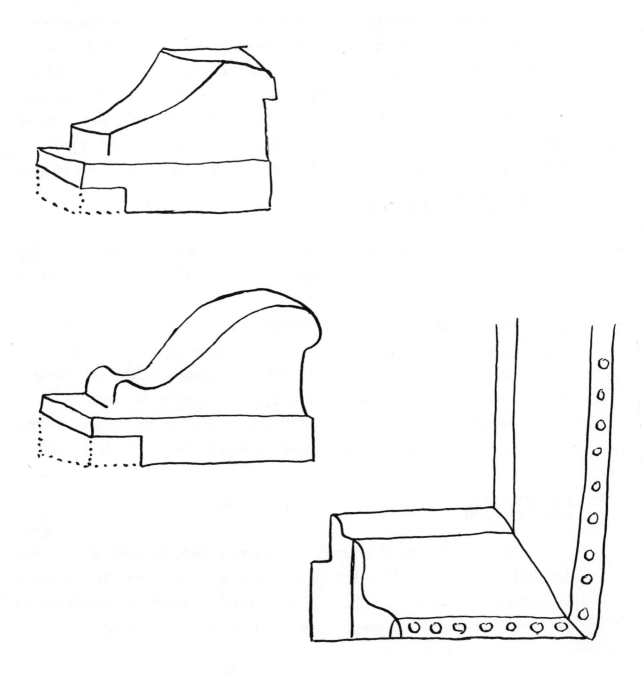

Many artists buy old frames at second hand stores and then stretch canvases to fit these frames. These old frames can be greatly improved by being painted a tone slightly off-white.

A wide frame (3½″ x 5″) is better for an oil painting than a narrow frame. But for water colors, narrow frames are usually better. Frames for water colors should be light and simple. Heavy frames and deep mouldings are much more appropriate for oil paintings.

When you are choosing a frame for a particular picture, select one that will show the painting to best advantage. Don't pick a frame that will compete with or detract from the painting. This may happen if the frame is too elaborate, or if the color in which the frame is painted clashes with the predominant colors in the painting itself.

Once an oil painting has been varnished, it does not require any additional protection against dirt and moisture. But water colors, since they cannot be preserved in this way, should be protected against the atmosphere by means of a sheet of glass.

HANGING PICTURES

Pictures look best when they are hung so that the center of the painting is at the eye level of a standing adult. Paintings should be hung flat; they should not be tilted.

The effect of the picture, after it has been hung, depends a great deal on the way the light falls on it. Because of the oil finish, light coming directly at the picture is not so satisfactory as light coming from above or from the side. This will eliminate glare and shine, which is especially important if the picture is varnished.

Instead of scattering a number of small pictures about the walls of a room, hang the paintings in a group, providing, of course, that there is no clash in subject matter or color.

CRITICISM

Never be discouraged by criticism. Listen to it, take what may be useful, and disregard the rest. You will find that most criticism is contradictory. No two people will tell you the same thing. If the artists of the past had completely believed all who were critical of their efforts, we should have very little great art today.

IMPATIENCE

Even if you have little time to paint, do not be impatient, because that is the greatest waster of time. Impatience is usually caused by a desire to complete the picture, but remember that the enjoyment and interest in all the phases of painting will give the most satisfactory result.